OLIVIA LASTING

LETTERS TO MY Child

ROCKRIDGE
PRESS

THIS JOURNAL IS FOR:

....

FROM:

....

Contents

Introduction

On the night I was born, my father sat in the hospital waiting room and wrote a six-page letter addressed to the child he was anxiously waiting to meet. He didn't know who I would become or how I would turn out, but he already loved me and wanted to put those feelings down on paper. He gave me that letter when I turned thirteen years old, and it's one of my most treasured possessions. In the years since then, that letter has stayed with me through thick and thin—through high school and university, multiple moves, parenthood, a flood, and all the other ups and downs of life.

I did not fulfill all the dreams my father had for me. Children rarely do; nor should we expect them to. But I have grown into a strong, successful, independent adult with two daughters of my own. Once I became a parent, I understood my father in a way I never had before. In the days following both my children's births, I wrote my own letters to them, documenting their birth stories and sharing my hopes and dreams for them. I plan to give them my letters when they finish high school, and I dearly hope they find my words as meaningful as I found my father's.

Every once in a while, I pull out my father's letter and read it again. Sometimes it's when I'm facing a challenge in my life and need encouragement. Sometimes it's when I need a reminder of his love for me. No matter the occasion, I come away feeling comforted and inspired. That sense of enduring comfort and love is my hope for you and your child as you make your way through this book.

You are holding the seeds of an extraordinarily valuable and unique gift for your own child. *Letters to My Child* will guide you in writing down your most personal thoughts, feelings, and dreams, and assist you in creating a meaningful family keepsake. In your letters, your child will feel your presence whenever they need it, even when you can't physically be with them.

How to Use This Book

This is a different kind of baby book. Instead of recording facts at predetermined times, this letter-based journal will help you exercise your creativity. As you reflect on meeting your child for the first time and your journey through parenthood, this book will guide you in documenting those special moments, milestones, family stories, and dreams that create connection and the deepest expression of your love.

Each page contains a prompt for a letter. The prompts are divided into four parts. The first part, "Welcome to the Family," will help you think back and reflect on the beginnings of your relationship with your child. In the second part, "Memorable Milestones," you'll be prompted to write letters recollecting important moments in your child's life. The third part features "Words of Wisdom," with prompts to draft letters to pass your best advice along to your child. And, finally, in "Hopes and Dreams for You," you'll pen your aspirations and dearest wishes for your child's future.

The beauty of this journal is its open-ended nature. Use this book in any way that feels right to you. That could mean working through the pages from start to finish, or you could flip through and choose a prompt that inspires you in the moment. At the end of each part there are lined pages titled "More Letters for You." Use this space to write down additional thoughts you want to share with your child, or to continue a letter from an earlier prompt. Keep this book at your desk or on your bedside table so it's available to write in whenever the mood strikes you. There are no expectations, no timeline, and no pressure.

Give your letters to your child when the time feels right. This might be on their sixteenth birthday, when they graduate from high school, when they leave home for the first time, or at the birth of their own child. Once passed on, these letters will be a record of your relationship, your family life, cherished memories, and words of wisdom that your child can take with them into the rest of their life.

welcome to the family

From the moment you find out your family is growing, your whole world becomes bigger, brighter, and more full of hope. Nothing can compare to the joy and anticipation you feel at the prospect of welcoming a new child! You might also feel overwhelmed by all the changes to come, and even a bit apprehensive as you think about how a new child will transform your life forever.

Use the prompts in this section to help you think back and record those first thoughts and reactions. Think about the day you first learned the news. Consider all the things you did to get ready and who celebrated with you. Remember how it felt when you finally welcomed your child into your family.

The day your child arrives changes you in ways you can't even begin to understand at the time. Writing down your thoughts in these pages will keep the memories fresh forever. Sharing these letters with your child in the future will help them appreciate the anticipation you felt as you waited for their arrival and the joy you felt at meeting them for the first time.

DATE ____ / ____ / ____

Dear ______________________,

I'll never forget what happened the moment I learned you would be joining our family. On the day I found out . . .

DATE ___ / ___ / ___

Dear ______________,

When I discovered you were on the way, I felt overwhelmed with so many big emotions all at the same time. I felt . . .

DATE ____ / ____ / ____

Dear ________________,

I was overjoyed at the news of your impending arrival, but I must admit I was also nervous about the future and how things would change. I worried about . . .

DATE ..... / ..... / .....

Dear .... ,

As soon as I learned you were on the way, I started to wonder what kind of parent I would become. I hoped that I would be . . .

....

....

....

....

....

....

Paste a photo of you perparing
for your child's arrival here.

DATE ..... / ..... / .....

CAPTION:

DATE ____ / ____ / ____

Dear ______________,

I couldn't wait to share my happiness that you would be joining our family, so I made an announcement by . . .

DATE ____ / ____ / ____

Dear ______________,

Friends and family members were thrilled by the news and eagerly anticipated meeting you for the first time. We celebrated your impending arrival by . . .

DATE ___ / ___ / ___

Dear ______________,

I wanted everything at home to be perfect and ready before your arrival. I prepared by . . .

DATE ___ / ___ / ___

Dear ____________,

Picking a name for you wasn't easy! There were a lot of things to think about before finally settling on the right one. I chose your name because . . .

DATE ____ / ____ / ____

Dear ______________,

I thought I knew what to expect, but when the day finally came, there were plenty of surprises. On that day . . .

DATE ____ / ____ / ____

Dear ____________,

I always knew that you would change my life forever, and I was right! The moment we first met, I realized that . . .

DATE ..... / ..... / .....

Dear ....,

The first time I held you in my arms and looked in your eyes, I fell deeply and instantly in love. All I could think was . . .

Paste an early photo of you and your child here.

DATE ..... / ..... / .....

CAPTION:

DATE / /

Dear ,

Your first day at home with me will always hold a special place in my heart. On that day . . .

DATE ____ / ____ / ____

Dear ______________,

Once you were home, I wanted so many of our friends and family to meet you! Your first visitors were . . .

DATE ____ / ____ / ____

Dear ____________,

The day you arrived changed my life forever, and I will always be grateful to the people who supported me and helped bring us together for the first time. Our strongest supporters were . . .

DATE / /

Dear ,

Those first few days with you were a blur of exhaustion and overwhelming emotions, but I never want to forget . . .

DATE ____ / ____ / ____

Dear ____________,

I had so many expectations for how things would go during those early days, but I didn't anticipate . . .

DATE ____ / ____ / ____

Dear ________________,

Our first few days and weeks together were full of wonderful discoveries. The most surprising thing I learned about you was . . .

DATE ____ / ____ / ____

Dear ____________________,

My favorite memory from those first few days and months is . . .

DATE ___ / ___ / ___

MORE LETTERS FOR YOU

DATE / /

DATE / /

MORE LETTERS FOR YOU

DATE / /

DATE / /

MORE LETTERS FOR YOU

DATE / /

DATE / /

MORE LETTERS FOR YOU

DATE / /

DATE / /

MORE LETTERS FOR YOU

DATE / /

memorable milestones

Take a few minutes to think about the meaningful moments that have marked your child's life and your relationship together. Remember that first sweet smile, the first word, the first tooth, the first step, and all the milestones that followed. Consider, also, the meaningful events as your child grew older, such as their first accomplishments at home and at school. What happened on your child's first day of school? How did you feel the first time they achieved a difficult goal, learned a special skill, or won an award? What was it like the first time you shared a beloved hobby together?

This section is an opportunity to record all those precious milestones and memorable "firsts" that you've been holding in your heart since your child's arrival. Consider ideas on the following pages to get you started, but above all else, make these letters as unique and personal as the relationship you have with your child. When you finally pass your letters along, your words will remind your child of their achievements and help them understand your enduring love and pride in their accomplishments.

DATE ____ / ____ / ____

Dear ______________,

We've shared a lot of firsts, but nothing compares to the first time you smiled at me. All I could think was . . .

DATE ..... / ..... / .....

Dear ....,

This is the very first photo of all of us together as a family. On the day this picture was taken, we . . .

....

....

....

....

....

....

Paste your first family photo here.

DATE ..../..../.....

CAPTION:

DATE ..... / ..... / .....

Dear ....,

It's hard to believe how small you were as a baby. But you grew so fast, and when I saw you take your first unsteady steps, I couldn't help but think . . .

DATE / /

Dear ,

I know you don't remember this, but I do! Here are the first foods you tried and what you thought about those new flavors . . .

DATE ___ / ___ / ___

Dear ____________,

I couldn't wait to hear your first words! I will never forget how excited I was when you finally said . . .

DATE ____ / ____ / ____

Dear ________________,

First birthdays are extra special. We invited ______________________________ to join
(guests)
us, and we celebrated your first birthday by . . .

Paste a photo from your child's first birthday here.

DATE ..../...../.....

CAPTION:

DATE ____ / ____ / ____

Dear ____________,

You were ________ years old when you finally learned to tie your shoelaces. I still remember how much you practiced and how proud you felt. If I tried to help, you would . . .

DATE ____ / ____ / ____

Dear ____________,

I will never forget the first time you saw the ocean/snow. You were utterly enchanted by the sight! We had so much fun playing . . .

DATE ...... / ...... / ......

Dear ....,

You've always been a kind and loyal friend. The first friend you made was ...., *(name)* and the two of you loved to play . . .

DATE / /

Dear ,

I'm not sure which one of us felt more nervous on your first day of school. I will always remember the little details of the day. You wore , and you told me . . .
(clothes)

DATE ____ / ____ / ____

Dear ________________,

Your first tooth fell out when you were ________________ *(age)*. Do you remember what happened when it fell out? You reacted by . . .

DATE ___ / ___ / ___

Dear ______________,

I remember how much you looked forward to your first party and how much fun you had.

It was for ______________________________, and you enjoyed . . .

(name/occasion)

DATE ____ / ____ / ____

Dear ______________,

You've accomplished a lot of things, but I will never forget how proud you were when you learned how to . . .

DATE ____ / ____ / ____

Dear ____________,

The first time you flew in a plane was when we visited ______________________________ .
(place/person)

I wanted flying to be a positive experience, so we prepared by . . .

DATE ..... / ..... / .....

Dear ....,

You were so proud of yourself the day you learned to ride a bike! You were a little bit wobbly when we first took off your training wheels, but then . . .

DATE / /

Dear ,

Family movie nights are always fun, but I'll never forget how excited you were the first time we saw your favorite movie . . .

DATE ____ / ____ / ____

Dear ________________,

Do you remember how hard I cheered for you at your first sports game/event? I loved seeing you play . . .

DATE ____ / ____ / ____

Dear ____________,

I wondered for years what it would be like when you started high school. When the first day of school came, I thought about . . .

DATE ____ / ____ / ____

MORE LETTERS FOR YOU

DATE / /

DATE / /

MORE LETTERS FOR YOU

DATE / /

DATE / /

MORE LETTERS FOR YOU

DATE / /

DATE / /

MORE LETTERS FOR YOU

DATE / /

DATE / /

MORE LETTERS FOR YOU

DATE / /

family adventures and stories

We all have favorite stories we love to tell over and over: stories about the cute things our kids said, funny family moments that make us laugh every time, memorable trips, and other occasions that brought us closer as a family. Think about how it feels to pass along these stories and how they bring the whole family together in shared laughter or tears.

This section will help you record and share those memories—moments that, though small, are precious. Stories like this are told and retold through the years, becoming part of our shared sense of family and belonging. No matter how big or how small, they bind us together and create fond memories we can think back on years later.

While you read through and respond to the prompts in this section, think about those funny, wild, sweet, and touching family stories you've been keeping tucked away in your heart. Once you write them down, your letters will connect your child to their roots and remind them of the shared stories and memorable moments that tie your family together forever.

DATE / /

Dear ,

I'm looking forward to going on many more grand adventures together. One of my favorite adventures with you was . . .

DATE ___ / ___ / ___

Dear ________________,

Your birthday is always a special occasion, but I especially remember the year we celebrated your birthday by . . .

DATE ____ / ____ / ____

Dear ______________,

When you were learning to communicate, there were some words you'd mispronounce and unique gestures you'd make. I smile every time I think about the adorable way you used to . . .

DATE ____ / ____ / ____

Dear ____________,

Holiday traditions have always been important in our family. I hope you'll never forget the time we all got together to celebrate . . .

DATE / /

Dear ,

I have countless funny family stories I love to tell, but the most hilarious story is the time you . . .

DATE ___ / ___ / ___

Dear ______________,

You are unique and wonderfully you, but sometimes you remind me of myself when I was your age. I remember the time . . .

DATE ....../....../......

Dear ....,

My favorite family vacation was the time we went to .... (*location*). Do you remember how much fun we had when we . . .

....

....

....

....

....

....

Paste a photo from your family vacation here.

DATE ....../....../......

CAPTION:

DATE ___ / ___ / ___

Dear ______________,

When you were little, your favorite toy was ______________________________.
(toy/game)

You would spend hours playing . . .

DATE ___ / ___ / ___

Dear ______________,

When you were little, your favorite books to read over and over again were . . .

DATE / /

Dear ,

I always enjoyed our nature adventures and spending time outdoors with you. Do you remember when we . . .

DATE ____ / ____ / ____

Dear ______________,

Your favorite food as a young child was ______________ *(food)*, but I remember there were certain foods you wouldn't even touch, like ______________ *(food)*. On one occasion . . .

DATE ___ / ___ / ___

Dear ________________,

I loved coming to your ______________________________ and cheering for you. I was
(games/recitals/performances)

so proud of your accomplishments and I loved watching you . . .

DATE ...... / ...... / ......

Dear ....,

Pets are family, too! Some of my favorite family memories involve our pets, like . . .

Paste a photo of
your pet here.

DATE ..../...../......

CAPTION:

DATE ___ / ___ / ___

Dear ______________,

You've always had a wonderful sense of humor and a contagious laugh! I remember the jokes and riddles you would tell, like . . .

DATE ____ / ____ / ____

Dear ____________,

When you were little, you had so many dreams and ideas about what you wanted to be when you grew up. I remember you used to tell me . . .

DATE ___ / ___ / ___

Dear ____________,

Change can be scary, but it can also be an opportunity for something new and exciting. You were so nervous when you had to change schools . . .

DATE / /

Dear ,

There are certain you-and-me moments we've shared that I will hold in my heart forever, like the time . . .

DATE ___ / ___ / ___

Dear ____________,

The way that families support each other through difficult and painful times helps make us stronger and brings us closer together. I will always cherish the memory of how we all came together when . . .

DATE / /

MORE LETTERS FOR YOU DATE / /

DATE / /

MORE LETTERS FOR YOU

DATE / /

DATE / /

MORE LETTERS FOR YOU

DATE / /

DATE / /

MORE LETTERS FOR YOU

DATE / /

words of wisdom

It has been said that a parent's job is to teach their children not to need them anymore, but the hardest part of that job is accepting when we've succeeded. As parents and caregivers, raising a helpless baby to become a compassionate and self-sufficient adult is the most challenging yet rewarding job in the world. We teach our children how to bathe themselves, dress themselves, and make friends. We help them with homework and teach them how to cook and clean up after themselves. But those are the easy tasks. It's infinitely more difficult and demanding to teach them the really important things, like kindness, integrity, common sense, and independence.

In this section, think about which lessons and words of wisdom are most important to pass on to your child. Use the prompts to guide you in writing down the rules for living and guidance you want your child to keep in mind as they grow into adulthood. What advice do you want them to remember and take with them into the rest of their lives? When you give your child these letters, they will receive a handwritten trove of life lessons, parental advice, and reminders of your care and wisdom. They'll have your love and guidance to refer to always, even when you can't be with them.

DATE / /

Dear ,

There are many things I wish I'd learned when I was younger. Now, with the benefit of my own experience, I want to pass along these three important lessons . . .

DATE ____ / ____ / ____

Dear ______________,

When you were little, I used to sing ______________________________ to you.
(song title)

I remember how warm and cozy those moments were. Do you still remember the lyrics?

DATE ____ / ____ / ____

Dear ____________,

Your favorite home-cooked meal when you were growing up was ____________ *(food)*. I've written down the recipe here so you'll always have a taste of home with you wherever you go.

DATE / /

Dear ,

I hope you will always be surrounded by people who love and support you. When it comes to friends, it's important to look for people who will . . .

DATE ____ / ____ / ____

Dear ________________,

Character matters, especially when things are difficult. There will be times when you might be tempted to take the easy way out, and I hope that you always remember the values and lessons you learned from your family . . .

DATE ____ / ____ / ____

Dear ____________,

Remind yourself that nobody's perfect. When things get hard and you're tempted to quit, tell yourself . . .

DATE ...../...../.....

Dear ....,

When I was growing up, my family taught me important values. I want to share them with you . . .

Paste a photo of your family of origin here.

DATE ..../..../.....

CAPTION:

DATE ___ / ___ / ___

Dear ____________,

I've found certain practical rules and guidelines invaluable in my life when it comes to money matters. When you're managing your finances, I hope you will keep in mind . . .

DATE ____ / ____ / ____

Dear ____________,

Driving is an enormous responsibility. Whenever you get behind the wheel, please remember . . .

DATE / /

Dear ,

You're likely to spend almost a third of your adult life working. When you're job hunting, I hope you'll consider . . .

DATE ____ / ____ / ____

Dear ______________,

May you have many opportunities in your life to travel the world, visit new places, and meet new people. During your travels, keep in mind . . .

DATE / /

Dear ,

You've only got one body, so please pay attention to your health. Eat well, stay active, and . . .

DATE ____ / ____ / ____

Dear ________________,

Whatever happens, remember that I love you always and forever. Whenever you feel sad or down, I want you to think about these words . . .

DATE ___ / ___ / ___

Dear ______________,

Whenever you are dating, I want you to keep this advice in mind when choosing the person whom you will trust with your heart . . .

DATE / /

Dear ,

No matter how busy you get, make time for the most important things in life, such as . . .

DATE ____ / ____ / ____

Dear ________________,

I don't know if I'll ever be ready for you to grow up and move out, but this is the life advice I want you to keep in mind when you're living on your own . . .

DATE ____ / ____ / ____

Dear ____________,

If you ever decide to have a child of your own, I want you to have the advice I found most useful when I became a parent . . .

DATE / /

Dear ,

If I could only give you one piece of advice to take with you throughout your life, it would be . . .

DATE / /

MORE LETTERS FOR YOU

DATE / /

DATE / /

MORE LETTERS FOR YOU

DATE / /

DATE / /

MORE LETTERS FOR YOU

DATE / /

DATE / /

MORE LETTERS FOR YOU

DATE / /

hopes and dreams for you

From the day you learn that your family will be growing, you begin to dream. You dream about what your child will look like, what their laughter will sound like, and how it will feel to hold them in your arms. You dream about who they will become and what the future might hold for them. These hopes and dreams may change as they grow through childhood, adolescence, and adulthood, but you never stop dreaming for them.

Before you start this section, take a few minutes and allow your imagination to run free. What character traits and qualities do you hope your child will come to possess? What do you dream they might accomplish? What wishes do you have for their future? Think about these hopes for your child, now and in the future, as you write in the following pages. When the time comes for you to pass along your letters, know that you will be offering your child notes of confidence, comfort, and inspiration they will treasure forever.

DATE ____ / ____ / ____

Dear ____________,

Before I even met you, I dreamed about the kind of family we would become. My dreams for you have changed in many ways since then, but I still believe . . .

DATE / /

Dear ,

I carry so many hopes and dreams for you in my heart. Most of all, I hope you will be . . .

DATE ___ / ___ / ___

Dear ____________,

Always be true to yourself. No matter what dreams I may have for you, my greatest wish is that you will follow your heart and pursue your own . . .

DATE ___ / ___ / ___

Dear ____________,

Believe in yourself as much as I believe in you. I believe you will . . .

DATE / /

Dear ,

In our family, we value qualities like kindness and compassion. I trust that you will also live by the values that matter most to you by . . .

DATE ____ / ____ / ____

Dear ______________,

Travel teaches us invaluable lessons about ourselves and the world around us. I would love for you to have the opportunity to visit . . .

DATE ..... / ..... / .....

Dear ....,

You can always count on your family, and I hope that you will always feel comfortable coming home. Remember, the door will always be open . . .

Paste a photo of the home (or one of the homes) where your child grew up.

DATE ..... / ..... / .....

CAPTION:

DATE ____ / ____ / ____

Dear ____________,

My wish for you is that you grow up to be strong, independent, and empowered to pursue your passions, no matter what they might be. May you . . .

DATE ____ / ____ / ____

Dear ______________,

You used to tell me you wanted to be a ______________ *(job/career/aspiration)*. Your dreams might change as you grow, but no matter what path you choose, I hope you will find meaning and satisfaction in your work. It might not always come from the places you expect, but . . .

DATE / /

Dear ,

Education is essential, whether it comes from school or from another source of knowledge. Stay open to new experiences and lifelong learning because . . .

DATE ____ / ____ / ____

Dear ________________,

I dream you will grow into a compassionate adult who stands up for what's right and speaks out for those who don't have a voice. Be the kind of person who . . .

DATE ___ / ___ / ___

Dear ____________,

As a parent, I want you to have more opportunities and more successes than I did, so you can . . .

DATE ___ / ___ / ___

Dear ______________,

May you always be surrounded by people who respect you, cherish you, and see your worth. I hope for you to have lifelong friendships and relationships that . . .

DATE / /

Dear ,

I hope you will find a life partner you can love wholeheartedly and share your life with.

I dream that this person will give you . . .

DATE ____ / ____ / ____

Dear ______________,

It's important to know how to let loose and relax. I hope you foster a sense of fun and joy in your life by . . .

DATE ____ / ____ / ____

Dear ______________,

When times are hard, I hope you will feel comfortable asking for help and offering help in return. Having people around to support you makes . . .

DATE ..... / ..... / .....

Dear ....,

I dream of a day when you're a parent yourself and we can share stories of parenthood with each other. I imagine us sitting down together and talking about . . .

Paste a photo of you
and your child here.

DATE ..... / ..... / .....

CAPTION:

DATE / /

Dear ,

If I could have three wishes for your future, I would wish for . . .

DATE / /

MORE LETTERS FOR YOU DATE / /

DATE / /

MORE LETTERS FOR YOU

DATE / /

DATE / /

MORE LETTERS FOR YOU

DATE / /

MORE LETTERS FOR YOU

DATE / /

Acknowledgments

This book was written for my father, who inspired my love of words, and for my daughters, who inspire everything else that I do. I hope that every time my children read my letters to them, they are reminded how much they are loved.

About the Author

Olivia Lasting is a writer, social worker, and mother of two living in Vancouver, Canada. She has been writing her entire life, most recently for her personal website, ThisWestCoastMommy.com. When she's not experimenting in the kitchen or filling up her camera with photos of her kids, you can find her watching '80s fantasy movies or staying up late with a mug of Earl Grey tea and a good book.

First Rockridge Press trade paperback edition 2022

For general information on our other products and services, please contact our Customer Care Department within the United States at (866) 744-2665, or outside the United States at (510) 253-0500.

Hardcover ISBN: 978-1-68539-962-7

Manufactured in the United States of America

Interior and Cover Designer: Brieanna Felschow
Art Producer: Janice Ackerman
Editor: Maxine Marshall
Production Editor: Jenna Dutton
Production Manager: Martin Worthington

Copyright Page: Illustrations © Pigment Café/Creative Market, © PeDe Designs /Creative Market; Shutterstock.com

10 9 8 7 6 5 4 3 2 1 0